THE PINK PALACE

Royal Hawaiian

WAIKIKI

ROYAL
HAWAIIAN
341
HONOLULU

Courtesy of DeSoto Brown, Honolulu

THE PINK PALACE

Royal Hawaiian
WAIKIKI

BY **STAN COHEN**

PICTORIAL HISTORIES PUBLISHING COMPANY, INC.
Missoula, Montana

LIBRARY OF CONGRESS CATALOG CARD NO. 86-62543

ISBN 0-933126-82-4

First Printing October 1986
Second Printing January 1988
Third Printing July 1989
Fourth Printing August 1991
Fifth Printing August 1993
Sixth Printing February 1997

TYPOGRAPHY Arrow Graphics, Missoula, Montana

COVER DESIGN Artmill

PRINTED IN CANADA BY D.W. FRIESEN, ALTONA, MANITOBA

COVER PAINTING Menu cover of the Opening Night, February 1, 1927.

BACK COVER Postcards from author's collection.

About the Author

The author of *The Pink Palace* is a native of West Virginia and a resident of
Missoula, Montana. He has been in the publishing business for 20 years and
is the author of 55 books, mainly on military history. He has also written three
other Hawaiian books, *East Wind Rain, A Pictorial History of the Pearl Harbor
Attack; Hawaiian Airlines, A Pictorial History of the Pacific's Pioneer Air Carrier,* and
The First Lady of Waikiki, A Pictorial History of Sheraton Moana Surfrider.

Contents

ROYAL HAWAIIAN HOTEL MANAGERS
1927 to 1993

NAME	TITLE	DATE
Arthur Benaglia	General Manager	Februrary 1927 to January 1945
John C. Fischbeck	Manager	January 1937 to January 1942
Warren B. Pinney	General Manager	February 1945 to March 1947
Cannon Lorimer	Manager	March 1947 to December 1947
John C. Fischbeck	General Manager	December 1947 to August 1957
Frank Swadley	Manager	November 1957 to January 1959
Howard C. Donnelly	Manager	July 1960 to March 1963
Joseph Filoni	Manager	March 1963 to March 1964
Alan Schnell	Manager	March 1964 to November 1964
George Bogar	Acting Manager	November 1964 to May 1965
Gerald McKenna	Manager	May 1965 to February 1968
John Brogan	General Manager	March 1968 to January 1971
Royal Treadway	General Manager	January 1971 to October 1971
Kai Herbranson	General Manager	October 1971 to August 1974
Joseph F. Hebert	General Manager	August 1974 to September 1986
Peter Thompson	General Manager	October 1986 to November 1988
Josef Haas	Acting Manager	November 1988 to January 1989
William T. Scalley	General Manager	January 1989 to April 1993
Ernest K. Nishizaki	General Manager	May 1993

Introduction

*T*HE WORLD HAS MANY great hotels. Throughout the Pacific Basin are famous and historical establishments such as the Imperial Hotel in Tokyo, the Raffles in Singapore, the Manila Hotel in Manila and the Royal Hawaiian in Honolulu. The Royal is a newcomer compared to the others; still, it was built in a time of great opulence and craftsmanship.

Built only a few years before the Great Depression, the Royal survived that turmoil. It also survived the years of the Second World War, when it was turned over to the Navy.

During those halcyon days of the 1930s, the Royal earned a solid reputation for quality and service that has lasted to this day. Hawaii was the place to go and the Royal was the place to stay and be seen. Everyone—from famous film stars and noted statesmen to ordinary citizens who could afford a trip on a Matson steamer and a stay at the hotel—was off to Hawaii.

The Territory was not to let them down—not with its splendid beaches, superb weather and magnificent scenery. And what better place to stay while enjoying paradise than the Royal?

Today, the Royal's lovely setting on famous Waikiki Beach has been overshadowed by a multitude of high-rise hotels and condominiums. Gone are the baggage handlers in Oriental dress, the melodious Royal Hawaiian Band and the glittering Hispano Suiza automobiles. Still, the style and reputation of "The Pink Palace" have remained.

This book traces the Royal's colorful history from its opening in 1927 to the present. Many photos are published here for the first time. Despite the hotel's relatively brief existence, its background is fascinating.

This book would not have been possible without the help of Ken Brewer and Jackie McBride-Tsukiyama of the hotel's sales department, Taeko Busk of its guest-relations department, and Joseph F. Herbert, former general manager. Former long-time employee Joe Fukuda kindly consented to a long interview, as did several other former employees. I obtained most of the photos from the Royal Hawaiian

Archives, the Hawaii State Archives and the UPI/Bettmann Newsphoto Archives. Also, thanks to DeSoto Brown of Honolulu and Ray de Yarmin of the Pacific Submarine Museum, Pearl Harbor. Color postcards are from my collection.

The cover artwork is a reproduction of the Royal's opening-night menu. Steve Smith of Missoula, Montana, edited the manuscript and Missoula's Arrow Graphics provided typesetting and design consultation.

Now, sit back and enjoy a journey into the past—a journey to an era that is gone, but not forgotten.

Stan Cohen

Bibliography

While no definitive history of the Royal Hawaiian Hotel has been written, the establishment has been mentioned in several Hawaiian books, newspaper stories and features. Public archives also contain information. The author consulted the following books and magazine articles for the information in *The Pink Palace*.

Allen, Gwenfread, *Hawaii's War Years*, University of Hawaii Press, Honolulu, 1945.

Acson, Veneeta, *Waikiki, Nine Walks Through Time*, Island Heritage Limited, Honolulu, 1983.

Brown, DeSoto, *Aloha Hawaii, 100 Years of Pictures from Hawaii's Most Famous Beach*, Editions Limited, Honolulu, 1985.

—————, *Hawaii Recalls, Selling Romance to America, Nostalgic Images of the Hawaiian Islands: 1910-1950*, Editions Limited, Honolulu, 1982.

Eyre, David W., *The Night They Opened The `Royal*, Honolulu Magazine, 1971.

Wisniewski, Richard A., *Hawaii: The Territorial Years, 1900-1959, A Pictorial History*, Pacific Basin Enterprises, Honolulu, 1984.

Worden, William L., *Cargos, Matson's First Century in the Pacific*, University Press of Hawaii, Honolulu, 1981.

PHOTO SOURCES: HA—Hawaii State Archives; RH—Royal Hawaiian Hotel; MS—Matson Steamship Co.; new photos by the author.

An aerial view of the Moana Hotel on September 9, 1920. The area to the extreme left would be the future site of the Royal Hawaiian. Kalakaua Avenue runs in front of the hotel. The Ala Wai Canal had not been built. The outlet of Apuakehau Creek can be seen just west of the hotel. U.S. Army Museum

CHAPTER ONE
Early Honolulu Hotels

Early Honolulu Hotels

THE ROYAL HAWAIIAN HOTEL is not the oldest hotel on Waikiki. In fact, it came along rather late in the early history of the famous beach. The Waikiki Beach area that we know today was the residence of the Hawaiian monarchy for hundreds of years.

In 1848, the Great Mahele (land division) created by Kamehameha III broke up the crown-owned land into private ownership. This created smaller parcels of land in Hawaii and eventually fostered development of the area. A large amount of the land in private ownership now belongs to the Bernice Pauahi Bishop Estate and Queen Emma Estate.

A hundred years ago, the Waikiki area was primarily a swampland with some agricultural production. It was also home to a few fishermen and well-to-do families with elegant beach homes.

As early as 1837, a hotel, the Hotel Waikiki, was opened. In the 1880s and 1890s several more were opened: the Sans Souci (1884), Park Beach (1888) and Waikiki Seaside (1894). These hotels serviced the trickle of tourists who were coming to the Islands by steamship.

Built in 1884 by Allen Herbert, the Sans Souci was named for Frederick the Great's palace, San Souci. The hotel actually was a series of small bungalows and soon became very popular. The bungalows were demolished during World War I.

The Waikiki Seaside Hotel was another popular hotel. In the late 1920s it would provide the site for the present Royal Hawaiian.

In fact, the present Royal Hawaiian Hotel is the second hotel on Oahu known by this name. In 1872, King Kamehameha V built a large hotel in downtown Honolulu at the corner of Hotel and Richards streets. It was known as the Hawaiian Hotel, but King Kalakaua renamed it the Royal Hawaiian—apparently to give it a royal flavor. By the early 1900s the hotel had lost some of its "royal" luster and much of its business to the more modern downtown hotel, the Alexander Young, and the Moana and Seaside cottages. The first Royal Hawaiian was converted to a YMCA building in 1917. The entire structure was demolished in 1926 and a new (present) YMCA building built.

In 1896 the Moana Hotel Co., bought a site on Waikiki Beach that was the residence of the Walter Peacock family. Hawaiian monarchs had been the earliest known residents of this site. A large, wood-framed hotel named the Moana was built and opened in March of 1901. The hotel was expanded in 1918 and was the premier hotel on the beach until the present Royal Hawaiian was opened in 1927. It still is operating under the ownership of the Kyo-ya Co. and is managed by ITT Sheraton Corporation.

Several other hotels were built in the sparsely populated Waikiki Beach area. The Hau Tree Hotel, now the Halekulani on Lewers Street, was the converted home of Robert Lewers. The Hau Tree opened in 1917 and the present hotel building was opened in 1983, incorporating a lobby built in 1931. In 1928 the Hotel Niumalu was built on the present site of the Hilton Hawaiian Village, which opened in 1956.

> *"The smart winter throng is gathering at Waikiki."*
> **Hawaii Tourist Bureau**

The first Royal Hawaiian Hotel in downtown Honolulu, now the site of the Army/Navy YMCA. HA

The Moana Hotel, just a few blocks from the Royal Hawaiian, is the oldest surviving hotel in Waikiki. HA

A good aerial view of the two hotels (Royal Hawaiian, left; Moana, right) on Waikiki Beach in 1931. Navy seaplanes are flying overhead. Quite a few houses apparently had been built in the Waikiki area by this time. UPI/Bettmann Newsphotos

CHAPTER TWO
Building the Hotel

Building the Hotel

*H*AWAII AND TOURISM are synonymous. That also was true in the 1920s, but to a lesser degree. Although one could travel to Hawaii aboard a Matson steamship or some other company's ship, the vessels were not overly attractive to the new rich who could afford overseas travel. Although a trip to Honolulu from the West Coast took about the same time as a transAtlantic trip to Europe, Hawaii-bound tourists traveled less comfortably. In Europe, one had the entire Continent to tour and enjoy; and there was the chance to hobnob with the elite on Riviera beaches.

Hawaii was a speck in a vast ocean, but it had several alluring features—magnificent weather, splendid beaches and beautiful scenery. It also was the gateway to exotic, far-away places in the South Pacific and the Orient.

America was experiencing unparalleled post-war prosperity in the early 1920s, with many people becoming wealthy through stock-market investments. It was a time of opulence, fancy cars, fast trains and an abundance of speakeasys and gin runners. It also was a time for some unscrupulous land speculation, especially in Florida and California. Swindlers sold property to people planning dream vacations.

Many years earlier, Captain William Matson, founder of the Hawaii-based Matson Navigation Co., had advocated a complete system of commodity-handling for his company. One example was to own oil wells, oil-storage tanks and ships to carry the oil to refineries.

A new commodity now appeared on Hawaiian shores. The commodity was tourists with money. What was needed was a grand cruise ship to get the tourists to Hawaii and a grand hotel in which to house them. The Matson management team of Edward Tenney and William Roth was determined to provide this service for the company's Hawaiian business empire as soon as possible. Tenney was president of Matson Navigation Co. and Castle & Cooke; Roth was Matson's manager and was married to William Matson's daughter, Lurline.

A new ship, the *Malolo*, was authorized for construction to carry passengers to Hawaii. A new hotel was proposed for construction on the beach at Waikiki. In downtown Honolulu, only two major hotels were

Those were the times of the Charleston and Prohibition. You kept your bottle of okolehao under the table.

Captain William Matson, founder of the Matson Steamship Co., builder and owner of the Royal Hawaiian Hotel. MS

William P. Roth, a former San Francisco stockbroker, married Lurline Matson. It was his idea to build a luxury hotel to go along with Matson's luxury cruise ship, the *Malolo*. MS

open in 1925—the Alexander Young and the Blaisdell. Neither was sufficiently opulent for the new clientele Matson would bring over on the *Malolo*. In the Waikiki area were three old hotels—the Moana and the Seaside Bungalows, owned by the Territorial Hotel Co. Ltd., and the Halekulani.

Castle & Cooke, one of Hawaii's big five financial companies, pledged $200,000 in 1924 for construction of a new hotel. A company was formed in 1925 incorporating Matson Navigation and Conrad C. von Hamm's Territorial Hotel Co. Castle & Cooke also was involved

The Kings resting place, "Helumoa," in 1863, site of the Royal Hawaiian Hotel. RH

and Edward Tenney was named to head the new company. Atherton Richards was treasurer; Alexander G. Budge was secretary; T.H. Pettrie and F.C. Atherton, both Castle & Cooke officials, were directors. The proposal was to spend $2 million on the hotel.

A 15-acre parcel was picked on Waikiki Beach—a site formerly used by Hawaiian royalty. King Kamehameha I had used the area as a playground after he conquered Oahu; Queen Kaahumanu had her summer palace in the coconut grove at the site. The purchase proved to be unpopular with many natives of the area. A 50-year lease was obtained from the Bernice Pauahi Bishop estate, owner of most real estate in the Waikiki area. Another 400 acres of the Waialae Beach area near Diamond Head was leased for a new golf course.

A North Dakota farm boy with an engineering background, Budge was hired by Tenney and Roth to make sure the hotel was built to their specifications. Budge joined Castle & Cooke in 1920 and managed that company's relations with Matson, but he knew nothing about building a resort hotel.

Arthur Benaglia was named the first manager of the Royal. He is in the center of the photo. He would guide the hotel through its first 18 years and establish the reputation of excellence that has endured. RH

Italian-born Arthur Benaglia was hired to manage the hotel. Benaglia had worked for many years in Canadian Pacific's resort-hotel chain. Before construction started, he and Budge toured the United States and Canada to examine resort hotels and to introduce Budge to the resort-hotel business. Benaglia would spend the next 18 years (except the war years) managing the Royal and making it one of the premier hotels of the world.

The widely known New York architectural firm of Warren and Wetmore was hired to design the hotel and draw plans. Unfortunately, the architect, Wetmore, did not visit the site before beginning; that would prove to be a costly mistake.

The architect had designed an odd-shaped building with one wing parallel to the beach. Construction began in October 1925 and would take almost 18 months to complete. Hundreds of workers were hired; and 35,000 barrels of cement, 75 miles of wire, 50 tons of stucco and

Construction progress during 1925 and 1926.
HA & RH

The architect and builders of the Royal conferring during the construction phase. HA

Garden side view of construction progress, probably late 1920. HA

Oceanside views of the construction. The hotel was
built of large sandstone blocks with a stucco finish. It
took approximately 18 months to finish construction.
HA

Driveway construction coming in from Kalakaua Avenue. HA

9,000 gallons of paint, stain and lacquer were used in what would be the largest building project in the Pacific area to that time.

When the hotel was nearing completion, the structure, except for the waterfront side, started to sink into the swampy areas the architect had been warned about. Before the Ala Wai Canal construction was started in 1921, much of the Waikiki area was very swampy. Many areas were unsuitable for building construction. One such site was the area the architect had picked to anchor a corner of the new hotel.

A retired Navy engineer was quickly summoned to save the hotel from sinking into the quicksand. The architect left pockets in the upright foundation columns to jack up if the hotel started to settle, but that failed to correct the problem. The engineer finally had to recommend that huge bridge-type girders be put underneath the structure and jacks used between the girders and the sinking columns. Large concrete blocks that were inserted in the columns still can be seen in the hotel's basement.

By now, the hotel cost had soared to $4 million. A nationally known landscape architect, R.T. Stevens, was hired to transform 12 acres of the hotel's grounds into a tropical paradise. Seth Raynor was retained to design an 18-hole golf course at the Waialae site. An advertis-

"The gardens are a wilderness of flowers and evergreen beauty with 40 varieties of plants. The tree ferns were imported from the Volcano House."

A good vertical view of the hotel under construction, probably in 1926. Kalakaua Avenue, now the main thoroughfare of Waikiki, is to the left. HA

Construction photo taken May 21, 1926. RH

ing agency was hired before the hotel construction even started to promote it throughout the world.

The Spanish-Moorish appearance of the building was quite unusual for this part of the world. But this was the 1920s and the influence of Spanish style was "in" on the mainland, partly as a result of Rudolph Valentino movies. The hotel also had overtones of the California mission style as seen in the cupolas or bell towers. Its 400 rooms were lavishly decorated and the theater-ballroom (now called the Regency Room) was decorated with images of barges floating down the Nile. An outdoor dining space (the Persian Room) was built where the Monarch Room is now situated. Many rooms had lanais, with louvered hall doors and Monel metal screens.

Rugs were imported from Czechoslovakia, Tunisia, Holland and Persia.

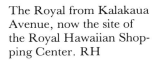

Rudolph Valentino was the rage at the time.

The Royal from Kalakaua Avenue, now the site of the Royal Hawaiian Shopping Center. RH

Entrance to main driveway off of Kalakaua Avenue in May 1927. This area now is occupied by the Royal Hawaiian Shopping Center. HA

A good pre-war aerial view of Waikiki Beach and the two famous beach hotels. The Outrigger Canoe Club is the low-lying building just off the northeast corner of the hotel. The long pier that jutted out into the water from the Moana Hotel has been removed. The Waikiki Theater, built in 1936, lies just to the north of the hotel. The Ala Wai Canal is in the background. HA

Benaglia was going to make this the finest hotel in the Pacific, if not in the world. His staff of 300 included 40 room boys, 20 bellboys, 10 elevator operators, five telephone operators, two doormen, two pages and eight Chinese lobby boys dressed in native costumes. His 60-member kitchen staff was assisted by 95 waiters serving the best of cuisine. Three men were employed full-time just to trim the 800 palm trees on the grounds. The idea was to prevent coconuts from falling on the heads of guests.

In 1934, the Territorial Hotel Co. Ltd., owner of the Royal and Moana hotels, the Seaside Bungalows, the Waialae Ranch Co. and Territorial Properties Ltd., was liquidated. Hawaiian Properties Ltd. took over these assets (the owners of both companies were mostly the same). Matson assumed full control of the hotels in 1941.

> **"The finest resort hostelry in America."**
>
> **Honolulu Star-Bulletin**

Seaside view showing the surf porch, which is now glassed in, and the corner of the building, which has been extended for The Surf Room. HA

The Porte Cochere, or main entrance to the hotel. The outside left column has been removed because of large vehicles hitting it. HA

Seaside view showing the old dining room, now the site of The Monarch Room. HA

Bamboo awnings were placed over all outside windows. HA

A view of Diamond Head, the Moana Hotel and its pier from the newly completed Royal. Landscaping is being done on the ocean side. HA

Landscaping work on the Coconut Grove entrance, January 1927. The fountain was removed years ago. HA

Looking south from the northwest corner of
Coconut Grove showing newly planted
ferns, January 1927. HA

HA

The driveway and parked cars in the area now occupied by the Royal Hawaiian Shopping
Center. HA

Views of the Presidential Suite, in which President Franklin D. Roosevelt stayed
on his overnight visit, July 14, 1934. UPI/Bettmann Newsphotos

Interior views of
rooms and suites in
the 1930s showing
typical furniture and
fixtures of the times.
HA

More interior
views. HA

The lower lobby facing the beach area was the entrance to both the Persian Room and the Ballroom. HA

The main lobby soon after the hotel opened. The registration desk on the left was moved to the opposite side of the lobby after the war. HA

The world-famous Coconut Grove Bar, now occupied by an art gallery just off the main lobby area, was converted to a soda fountain during the war years. HA

The elevators just off the main lobby soon after the hotel opened. HA

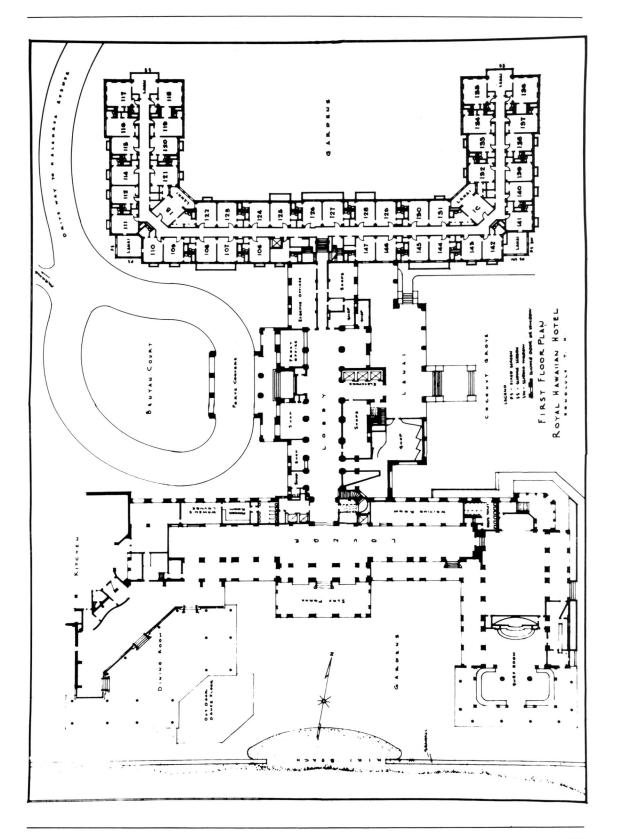

First Floor Plan
Royal Hawaiian Hotel
Honolulu, T. H.

The main ballroom, now the Regency Room, was the scene of many elaborate functions in its day. The Surf Room has since been built, extending from the far end. The large windows on the left side have been closed off by a walled-in walkway. HA

The lanai facing Coconut Grove was much larger in the old days. Part of it was closed-in years ago and now is occupied by a clothing store. HA

The elegant main dining room, originally costing $350,000, was situated on the southwest corner of the hotel. It was torn down during the post-war reconstruction and the present Monarch Room was built. Giant pillars held up a massive roof and large chandeliers were suspended from the ceiling. The new dining room is completely glass-enclosed with an outside dance floor. HA

The original dining room, called the Persian Room, now the site of The Monarch Room, was filled to capacity for the $10-a-plate black-tie dinner and ceremonies. HA

CHAPTER THREE
Opening Night

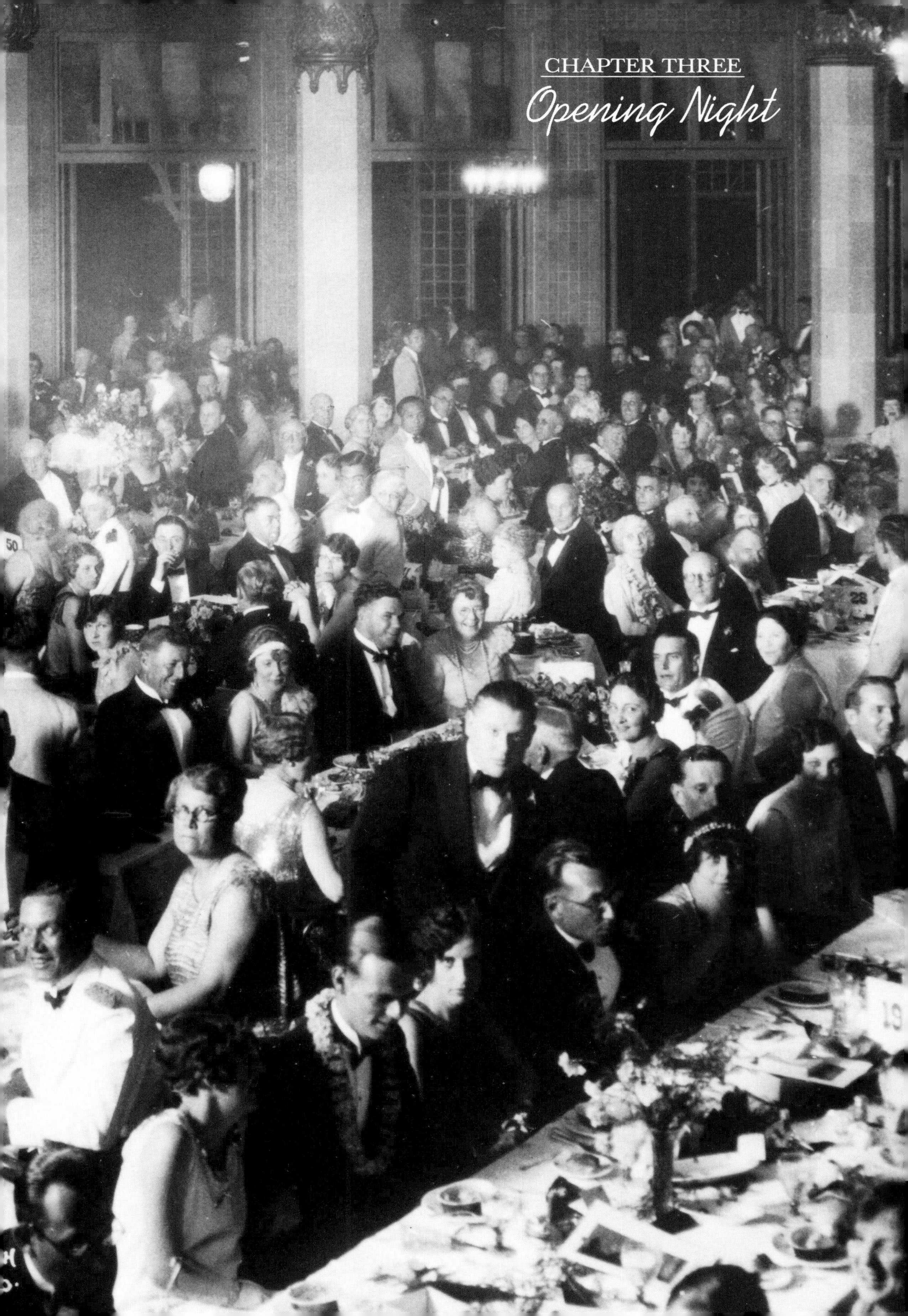

Opening Night

ON JANUARY 31, 1927, the *Honolulu Star-Bulletin* published a special 80-page edition to celebrate the grand opening of the Royal Hawaiian Hotel on February 1. It called the hotel "the finest resort hostelry in America" and cited "a new recreation era," adding that Hawaii would become a "playground of the Pacific." The edition went on to describe every detail of the hotel from its lavish gardens to the pin cushions in each room. After all, this was to be the major event of the year in Honolulu; 1,200 people, including Territorial Governor Wallace R. Farrington, paid $10 a plate to take part in the ceremonies. Tickets were at a premium for this gala event and Loraine Kuck, then the society editor for the *Star-Bulletin*, listed the name of each guest and what the women were wearing. The widely known Honolulu couple, Mr. and Mrs. Walter Dillingham, brought a party of 78.

With the exception of Princess Abigail Kawananakoa and a few other native Hawaiians, the party was strictly a Caucasian affair. A 14-person concert orchestra from the Honolulu Symphony played chamber music during the dinner hour. (The group was so popular that the hotel management retained it for regular Saturday night dances.)

It was a black-tie dinner affair lasting two hours. The menu was as lavish as the hotel's decor. Featured were Coupe Czarine, Jordan Almonds, celery hearts, mixed olives, green-turtle soup Kamehameha, Supreme of Mullet Albert, medallions of sweet breads Wilhelmina, mousse of foie gras princesse, squab-chicken casserole Mascotte, salade Lurline, Royal Hawaiian givree, gourmandise and moka.

It would be a dinner long-remembered in Hawaii.

The opening ceremonies began at 9:30 p.m. with an hour-long pageant arranged and directed by Princess Kawananakoa. (A descendant of the former monarchy, she was the first registered guest although she did not stay overnight.) The pageant was staged just outside what is now The Monarch Room.

Honolulu newspapers trumpeted the grand opening. Included was an 80-page special edition of the *Honolulu Star-Bulletin*. Honolulu Star-Bulletin

The grand ball was attended by some 1,200 people who danced to the music of the Royal Hawaiian Band. HA

The *Star-Bulletin* called the pageant both "colorful and semi-barbaric," perhaps overly strong words for a production that depicted the arrival of King Kamehameha the Great to Oahu. It included a fleet of 15 canoes carrying fierce warriors, oarsmen and kahili bearers. Kamehameha was greeted by five princesses as he stepped ashore. Each princess represented one of the major Hawaiian Islands. Gladys Brandt was the princess from Oahu, Zena Schuman from Kauai, Eloise Fernandez Choice from Maui, Josephine Hopkins from Hawaii and Thelma Perry from Molokai. The king then sat on a throne and watched a program of native dances and chants.

After the show, guests danced in the ballroom until the wee hours of the morning.

The dinner and the entire evening would live on in memory for years.

The luxury ship *Malolo*, built by Matson to bring wealthy tourists to Hawaii and the Royal, was supposed to be ready for the hotel's grand opening in February. Launched in 1926 at the Camp shipyards in Philadelphia, she was to be the epitome of liners: 582 feet long, seven decks, two theaters, a gymnasium, a swimming pool and room for 650 first-

class passengers. She also had a telephone in each room, 100 complete private baths, 50 private showers and hot and cold fresh and saltwater taps in each room. With 25,000 horsepower developed by her engines, she could cruise at 21 knots and make the San Francisco-to-Honolulu run in 4½ days.

Malolo truly was a magnificent ship.

Unfortunately, on her trial run, she rammed into another ship. Damage exceeded $500,000. This delayed her sailing until well into 1927; when she finally did put to sea, she developed a tendency to roll — a trait that gave her owners constant problems.

Finally, on November 21, 1927, ten months after the Royal opened, the *Malolo* steamed into Honolulu's harbor. She stayed there for two days, went to Hilo for a few days, then returned to Honolulu, where a great banquet was held in her honor at the Royal.

Matson now could transport wealthy tourists from the mainland to Hawaii and back. And it had a luxurious hotel to house them while in Hawaii.

Unfortunately, the stock market crash two years later would upset these plans somewhat.

ROYAL HAWAIIAN HOTEL

Opening Night Guests
February 1, 1927

A large, hard-bound book with the signatures of every guest at the opening dinner is on display in the Royal's general manager's office. RH

Table
Number 9

Autographed

Name

Mrs. Joy. Elliott,

D. Marpole.

Mrs. O. L. Lange

Miss K A La Rue

D. F. Stace

Mary M. Marpole.

W. M. Wedric...

Oliver S. Lange. M...

This card is to bound in a...

February
1st 1927

l Hawaiian Hotel
Honolulu, Hawaii

l of Guests at the Opening Dinner

Address   City

Kailani Ave.   Henolulu.

ancouver, B. C.   Canada

ancouver BC   Canada

lgary   Canada

rand Rapids Mich   USA

ancouver B.C.   Canada

and Mc Alley Mississiffi   U.S.A.

Vucaver B C   Canada

Princess Kawananakoa was the first guest to register, although she did not stay overnight. Here, she is being serenaded at the front desk. RH

REGISTRATION CARD
ROYAL HAWAIIAN HOTEL
HONOLULU

Name *Princess David*
Kawananakoa

Address *Honolulu Hawaii*

Room No.

Rate

Card No **1**   Arrival Date *2.1.27*   B L D Ldg
Departure Date   B L D Ldg

REGISTRATION CARD
ROYAL HAWAIIAN HOTEL
HONOLULU

Name *Major & Mrs Douglas King*

Address *London. England.*

Room No. *374. 376. 376A-378-380*

Rate **1** Arrival Date **FEB 1 1927** B L D Ldg

Card No Departure Date B L D Ldg

Major and Mrs. Douglas King of London, on their honeymoon trip, were the first guests to check into the hotel at 11:30 a.m. on February 1, 1927. They moved over from the Moana Hotel with their maid and valet. They were assigned rooms 374, 376, 376A, 378 and 380 — ample space for the Kings and their servants. They returned almost every year until the beginning of World War II. Behind the desk is Fred R. Goodall, chief clerk. HA

Barbed wire was placed along Waikiki Beach soon after the Pearl Harbor attack to guard against a possible Japanese seaborne invasion. Martial law went into effect on December 8, 1941, and was to remain until October 24, 1944, when the threat of invasion had long since diminished in the Islands. HA

Royal Hawaiian at War

Royal Hawaiian at War

$\mathcal{S}$OON AFTER THE DECEMBER 1941 Pearl Harbor attack, the Navy Recreation and Morale Office leased the Royal Hawaiian, turned out the guests and transformed the hotel into a major rest-and-relaxation center for Navy personnel—mostly from the submarine service. The hotel's exterior was not substantially changed except for barbed wire stretched along the beach; the interior was altered considerably. The Coconut Grove cocktail bar became a soda fountain and the swank beauty salon became a dispensary. The tennis court became a basketball court and a baseball diamond was laid out on the grounds. The hotel company agreed to maintain the landscaping, the Navy paid for everything else. The garden staff was reduced to a dozen but kept up the beauty of the gardens throughout the war.

Sailors averaged 10-day stays at the hotel. Three men were assigned to a room, a far cry from the tight quarters of a submarine. Officers paid $1 a day, an enlisted man could stay for 25 cents.

The hotel was an ideal place for the submariners, who had spent many months on war patrols all over the Pacific. Sometimes the rowdy submariners would let off a little too much steam, but the hotel survived the cigarette burns and occasional knife cuts in the floors and doors. Clothes hanging out the windows to dry were a sign of the times.

The monthly lease by the Navy amounted to $17,500; this take-over period lasted for more than 3½ years.

Facilities of the Waialae Golf Club, along with many other hotels and resorts around the Islands, were made available to the armed forces. The Moana Hotel remained open as a guest hotel and was full all the time.

Joe Fukuda, a long-time employee of the hotel and a man of Japanese descent, said that all housekeeping was done by non-Japanese during the war. Since he was in the engineering department, he was retained as an essential worker. He remembers that during the early part of the war, a blackout was in effect from 6 p.m. to 6 a.m., but this gradually was eased. In December 1943, rooms facing the ocean had blackout restrictions lifted; all blackout regulations were lifted in July 1944.

The famous Royal Hawaiian Band, which had performed for the arrival and departure of ships at the Honolulu dock, gave concerts at defense areas, service posts and hospitals. The band also presented noon-hour concerts at the palace grounds, and after blackout restrictions were lifted, offered early-evening concerts in the parks.

The war ended in September 1945 and the Navy returned the hotel to the Matson Navigation Co. on October 31 of the same year. It took more than a year, more than $2 million of Matson's money and 600 construction workers to restore the hotel to the company's specifications. The interior was gutted and new floors, doors and windows added. The lobby was changed to its present arrangement and the old dining room (Persian Room) was demolished and the present Monarch Room rebuilt in its place.

Warren Pinney replaced Arthur Benaglia as general manager and removed the old iron beds, wicker-rattan furniture and flower-chintz decor. Hardwood furniture, solid-colored fabrics and terrazzo blocks to replace the tile floors were ordered by Pinney.

The old wine cellar in the basement, closed at the beginning of the war still stocked with liquor and champagne, was reopened to the delight of the hotel's management. The only door to the cellar had been sealed to make it look like part of the foundation; Navy officials never knew what they had locked up.

Twenty years to the day after the hotel first opened on February 1, 1927, the Royal reopened with a gala celebration.

Courtesy Pacific Submarine Museum

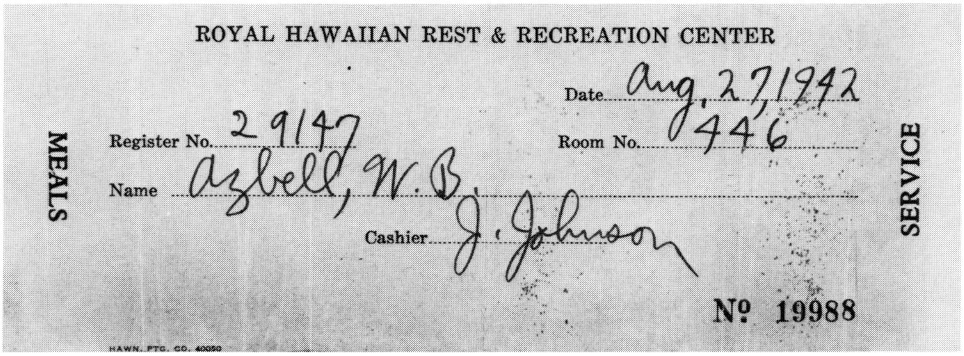

ROYAL HAWAIIAN REST & RECREATION CENTER

MEALS

Date Aug. 27 1942

Register No. 29147

Room No. 446

Name Azbell, W.B.

Cashier J. Johnson

SERVICE

№ 19988

HAWN. PTG. CO. 40050

ROYAL HAWAIIAN

RETURN PASS

OCTOBER 25

Unauthorized use of this pass will result in disciplinary action.

Front and back of a pass issued to all sailors staying at the hotel. Curfew was in effect after 2200 hours (10 p.m.). Pacific Submarine Museum

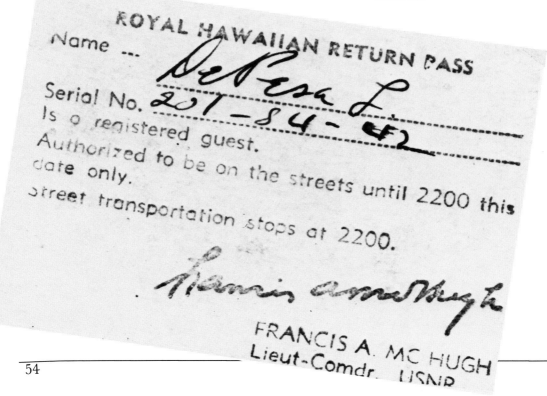

ROYAL HAWAIIAN RETURN PASS

Name ... *DePesa L*

Serial No. 207 – 84 – 42

Is a registered guest.

Authorized to be on the streets until 2200 this date only.

Street transportation stops at 2200.

FRANCIS A. MC HUGH
Lieut-Comdr. USNR

Sailors relaxing on the beach after returning from duty in the Pacific theater. Army Museum, Honolulu

Sports activities on the lawn.
UPI/Bettman Newsphotos

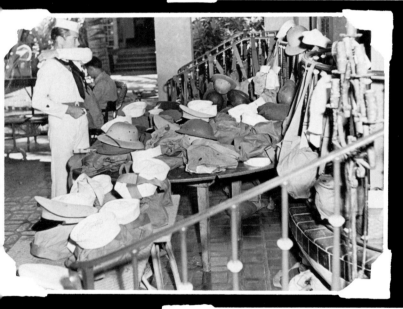

Tables piled high with helmets, caps and gas masks, which servicemen have tossed off to better enjoy the hotel's facilities.
UPI/Bettmann Newsphotos

The Coconut Grove cocktail bar was turned into a soda fountain.
UPI/Bettmann Newsphotos

The hotel, leased by the U.S. Navy in January 1942, provided a rest-and-relaxation center for submariners coming off months of Pacific war patrols.

UPI/Bettmann Newsphotos

Dancing was among many activities servicemen enjoyed.

UPI/Bettmann Newsphotos

Sailors on R&R on the beach in front of the hotel, 1942 or 1943. Bathers had to contend with ever-present barbed wire. UPI/Bettmann Newsphotos

The Navy still was in charge of the hotel in this 1945 photo. Remodeling had not begun on the Coconut Grove entrance. HA

By the time this photo was taken on September 25, 1945, the barbed wire was gone from the beaches and an air of normalcy had returned to the Islands. The hotel would not be opened to the general public for another two years. The Outrigger Canoe Club can be seen next to the hotel. HA

The old dining room (Persian Room) was demolished and the present Monarch Room built in its place.

Reconstruction of the hotel to return it to its pre-war elegance began in the fall of 1945. It would take almost two years to finish the work, with the official grand re-opening taking place on February 1, 1947.

The intricate roof patterns of The Monarch Room during construction in October 1946.

All photos from Hawaiian Archives

The Ocean Lanai was redone.

The lower lobby was gutted and the tile floor replaced by the present terrazzo.

Work also was done on the Coconut Grove entrance.

Chick Daniels, Warren Pinney Jr. and Renny Brooks count down the days until the reopening of the hotel on January 23, 1947. *Honolulu Advertiser*

Waikiki Beach, 1930s. Author's Collection

Waikiki Beach, Honolulu

Enjoying the Good Life

*A*H, THE GOOD LIFE, and it was good at the Royal. Before the Royal was built, hotels in Honolulu merely provided shelter. Tourists pretty much were on their own. But with the opening of the Royal Hawaiian in 1927, tourists were catered to with all the innovations the hotel's management could devise.

Guests could partake of ample recreational facilities on the grounds such as archery, lawn bowling, tennis, badminton or golf at the nearby Waialae Golf Course. Or, they could just stroll through the luxurious gardens. The beach, cordoned off for hotel guests, was, of course, the primary attraction. One could soak up the sun, ride on surf boards, play water polo, ride in an outrigger canoe or converse with the Royal Hawaiian Beach Patrol.

The front office could arrange a visit to a pineapple cannery, deep-sea fishing excursions, an automobile sight-seeing trip around Oahu, or even ukulele and hula lessons. Events of the day in the 1930s included Hawaiian serenaders and the Royal Hawaiian Girls' Glee Club in the dining room, coconut palm tree- climbing by native Hawaiians, a concert by the famous Royal Hawaiian Band under the direction of Harry Owens, and dancing in the ballroom after dinner.

The kitchen staff of the Royal prepared superb meals, as evidenced by 1930s menus. Special parties and dinners could be arranged with specially prepared menus. Guests wanting to try Japanese or Chinese cuisine were advised of the best restaurants in the Honolulu area.

Shops in the lobby catered to guests' every need, from the most fashionable outfits of the day to local souvenirs.

The hotel was the playground for the rich and famous—even in the dark days of the Depression of the 1930s. Matson brought over shiploads of wealthy tourists on its steamers, although the Depression severely curtailed the numbers until late in the decade. By 1936, Pan American Airways was beginning its weekly Clipper flights from California to Manila with a stop-over in Honolulu. This was an alternative to the 4½-day trip, but it was an expensive air trip and the Martin Clipper planes could carry only a few dozen passengers at a time.

Still, the good times were here for anyone who could afford them.

The Royal was to be the temporary home of presidents, royalty, actors, sports stars and well-heeled people in general all through the decade of the 1930s and into the early 1940s.

Names on the register included Mary Pickford and Douglas Fairbanks, who on a global tour stated that Honolulu was the most beautiful place in the world; the Rockefellers, the Fords, duPonts, Clark Gable, Al Jolson, Henry J. Kaiser, the Shah of Iran and many other Hollywood personalities, monarchs, politicians and financiers.

In those early days, guests usually would stay longer than visitors of today. They would come with their steamer trunks and even their servants. In the era before rental cars, many guests would bring their own personal cars on Matson's steamships.

In the first five years of operation, 14,000 guests stayed at the hotel. The peak year for tourists in Hawaii was 1929, with more than 22,000 visitors. The Great Depression caused a drop to a low of 10,000 in 1932 and 1933, and the number did not reach 22,000 again until 1936.

The era of opulence came to an abrupt end on the morning of December 7, 1941, when Japanese planes flew near Waikiki Beach on their way to the U.S. fleet berthed at Pearl Harbor.

Hispano Suizas, valets, steamer trunks....

The Hula is as Hawaiian as the palm tree and pineapple. RH

Many wealthy patrons brought elegant cars when they visited the Islands. This is a Hispano Suiza owned by Mr. and Mrs. Henry H. Rogers Jr. RH

The SS *Malolo*, Matson's
finest luxury steamer,
which brought elegant
tourists to Hawaii and the
Royal. HA

Even in the Depression
years of the 1930s, some
people still had the means
for elegant living. RH

Swimming and sun-
bathing were the prime at-
tractions of Waikiki Beach
and gave it its world-
famous reputation. HA

Playing surfboard polo on
a crowded day at the
beach. HA

Surfing with sails was
another popular pre-war
sport on Waikiki Beach.

The Waikiki Beach Patrol, May 1935. Left to right: John Maku, Sam Kaluhiokalani, Charles Bapasti, Ted Waters, Chick Daniels, Harry Cornwell, Pua Kealoha, "Sally" Hale and Joe Miner. HA

Surfers and beach boys with trophies in front of the Royal, 1930. HA

Harry Owens and his
Royal Hawaiian Band.
RH

Courtesy of
DeSoto Brown,
Honolulu

Harry Owens and his Royal Hawaiian Orchestra were very popular and widely known around the Islands. He wrote songs and invented a dance called the Oni-Oni (opposite). Owens' orchestra included violin players Robin McQuesten (left), Tony Perrotti and singer Ray Kinney. HA

An austere Royal Hawaiian Orchestra played each evening at dinner in the dining hall in the 1920s. The wall in front of the orchestra no longer exists. *Honolulu Star-Bulletin*

HONOLULU HONOLULU

ROYAL HAWAIIAN HOTEL
AND
MOANA-SEASIDE HOTEL & BUNGALOWS

Ancient Hawaii had no word for "Weather"

OFFICIAL AVERAGE TEMPERATURE
(U. S. Weather Bureau)

Jan.	71.0	July	77.8
Feb.	71.0	Aug.	78.4
Mar.	71.5	Sept.	78.2
Apr.	73.1	Oct.	77.0
May	74.9	Nov.	74.6
June	76.6	Dec.	72.5

HAWAIIAN HOTELS, LIMITED
HONOLULU, HAWAII
Cable and Radio Address:
Royal Hawaiian "ROYALHOTEL"
Moana-Seaside "MOANA"

ROYAL HAWAIIAN HOTEL
AND
MOANA-SEASIDE HOTEL & BUNGALOWS

HAWAIIAN HOTELS, LIMITED
HONOLULU, HAWAII
Cable and Radio Address:
Royal Hawaiian "ROYALHOTEL"
Moana-Seaside "MOANA"

Courtesy of DeSoto
Brown, Honolulu

ROYAL HAWAIIAN HOTEL, TROPICAL GARDENS, HONOLULU, T. H.

ROYAL HAWAIIAN HOTEL AT NIGHT, HONOLULU

COPYRIGHT P. P. HONOLULU

4A-H790

Afternoon tea in the lower lobby. The hostesses wear Japanese kimonos, a practice curtailed after December 1941. HA

Ladies luncheon on the Coconut Grove lanai, 1930s. The far end of the lanai now is occupied by a clothing store. HA

ROYAL HAWAIIAN HOTEL

~ Menu ~

Hors d'Oeuvres Assortie

Queen Olives   Almonds

Borstch a la Russe   Creme de Volaille Reine Blanche

Supreme of Ulaula a la Tremine

Noisette of Spring Lamb, Cendrillon
Partridge in Casserole Alcantara

Punch Marquise

Farm House Capon Bread Sauce
Young Suckling Pig, Apple and Raisin Stuffing
Guava Jelly   Candied Yams

String Beans Tourangelle   Baby Lima Beans in Butter
Dauphine Potatoes

Salad Eliza

Hawaiian Palm Leaves   Moka Butter Slice
Frozen Peach Delice au Sabayon
Desire de Dames
Demi Tasse

January 1st. 1928   Honolulu.

DINNER

Grapefruit Montmorency

Canape Caviar Frais   Mixed Olives
Salted Almonds

Celery en Branche

Consomme aux Nids d'Hirondelle
Veloute de Volaille Dame Blanche

Paupiette de Mahimahi Boieldieu
Langouste Cardinal

Filet of Beef Poelee Brehan

Native Turkey Chestnut Dressing, Cranberry Sauce
Sorbet Anissette

Braised Celery Troubadour   Broccoli Polonaise
Potatoes   Darphin

Royale

Parfait de Foie Gras a la Gelee de Porto
Aristocrat

Cream Doria in Jelly Romanoff
Goteaux Louis XIV   Pear on Rice Conde
Butter Palm Leaves

Coupe Colinette

THURSDAY, JANUARY 1st, 1931

HONOLULU, HAWAII

The Royal Hawaiian Ensemble

New Year's Day Program

Eight-thirty o'clock

1. Nights of Gladness - - - Ancliffe
2. Oriental Sketch "Among the Arabs" - Langey
3. Dreams - - - - Strelezki
4. Kamenoi Ostrow "Cloister Scene" - Rubenstein

Intermission

5. Moszkowskiana, from the works of Moszkowski
6. Indian Plaint - - - - Dvorak
7. Schon Rosemarin - - - Kreisler
8. Selection from "Pagliacci" - Leoncavallo

Under direction of Claire Rogers Cleghorn

79

At the site of the original 1927 nursery, a recreational area was set up with lawn bowling, archery and tennis courts. HA

Swinging porch chairs were set up on the Ocean Lanai. RH

Members of an Oakland, California, Chamber of Commerce tour group on their arrival at the hotel in the 1930s. RH

A fashion show in The Monarch Room. RH

The first baggage
handlers were dressed
in typical Oriental
dress. RH

The first bellboys.
RH

Koko Head.

COCKTAILS • Special • Royal Hawaiian Cocktail

LUNCHEON

Pineapple Juice, Fresh Island Tomato Juice or Poi Cocktail

Green Onions   Chow-Chow   Herring Delicatessen   Garden Radishes
Pickled Walnuts   Imported Salami Sausage   Celery Root Julienne
Italian Plate   Carrots & Cabbage Slaw

SOUP

Consomme Vermicelli   Chicken Okra Creole
Consomme, Essence of Tomato or Chicken Broth in Cup, Hot or in Jelly

FISH

Broiled Hawaiian Lobster Paprika Butter with Rice Oriental

ENTREES

Shirred Eggs Chaumiere
Quartered Egg Bordelaise
Calf Liver Saute with Smothered Onions
Navarin of Spring Lamb aux Primeurs
Smoked Loin of Pork with Lentils
Vegetable Plate with Green Pepper
Fried Polenta

PAPAI HAUPIA "COLD HAWAIIAN CRABMEAT"
Fruit Luncheon Plate, Royal Hawaiian

FROM THE GRILL

Broiled Minute Steak, O'Brien Potatoes

STRICTLY FRESH VEGETABLE

Chopped Spinach   Corn on the Cob, Melted Butter   Buttered Beets
Summer Squash   Wainaku Lehua Poi   Boiled Rice
Potatoes—Special Baked, Mashed, New Boiled Haw'n Rose or Long Branch

COLD BUFFET

Roast Spring Chicken   York or Prague Ham
Galantine of Capon in Jelly   Ox Tongue   Prime Ribs of Island Beef
Pressed Chicken & Virginia Ham in Jelly   Veal Loaf, Potato Salad
Spring Lamb with String Beans Salad

SALAD

Red & Green Cabbage Slaw   Alligator Pear   String Beans, Country Style
Island Lettuce, 1000 Island Dressing
VITAMIN: Jul of Cabbage, Lettuce, Tomato, Jul of Calf Liver,
Chives, Watercress, hard boiled Egg, Royal Dressing

A BIT OF SWEET MAKES THE MEAL COMPLETE
DESSERT AND ICE CREAM

French Pastry   Vanilla Custard Pie   Fresh Apple Pie
Hot Mince Pie   Raisin Pudding   Pumpkin Pie
Peach, Coffee, Chocolate or French Vanilla Ice Cream
From our own Grove, Cocoanut Ice Cream

FRESH FRUIT

Grapes   Apples   Banana   Papaia   Pineapple   Oranges   Figs
Strawberries   Bartlett Pears   Persimmons   Casaba & Watermelon
Tangerines

CHEESE

Schabzieger Philadelphia Cream   Old English   Camembert   Cottage
AFRICAN DATES   NUTS & RAISINS
COFFEE   TEA   MILK

ANY DISHES ORDERED THAT ARE NOT ON THE MENU WILL BE CHARGED EXTRA
ROOM SERVICE, 25c EXTRA EACH PERSON.

EGGS CREAM & MILK SUPPLIED BY OUR OWN RANCH & DAIRY
HONOLULU, HAWAII   THURSDAY JANUARY 4 1934

To Our Patrons

Our kitchen is equipped to prepare at moderate prices any special dishes you may desire.

Please leave your orders with our maître d'hotel for parties and dinners with specially prepared menus.

Kindly ask the head waiter for souvenir menu ready for mailing.

THE INFORMATION DESK is located in the lobby where arrangements may be made for Sports Activities and Motor Tours.

THE WAIALAE GOLF COURSE offers you the finest 18-hole golf links in The Territory. Completely equipped clubhouse. Ted Benedict, Professional Green fees $2.00 on week days, $2.50 on Saturdays, Sundays and Holidays. Monthly rates quoted.

TENNIS. The Moana-Seaside Courts are available to Guests of the Royal Hawaiian Hotel. Courts may be reserved through the Front Office.

A visit to the Pineapple Cannery is interesting. Please see the Clerk at Desk.

A few of the finest instructors of the HULA have been especially engaged for the benefit of our guests.

We are glad to recommend to our guests wishing to have Japanese or Chinese dinners:

IKESU, Ala Moana Road (Sukiyaki dinner in quaint Japanese setting. Geisha entertainment)

LAU YEE CHAI, Kalakaua Avenue (Chop Sui House - Finest Chinese cooking - Immaculate cleanliness - Typical background)

EVENTS OF THE DAY - PRESENTED BY JOHNNY NOBLE

AFTERNOON TEA SERVED ON WAIKIKI LANAI   3:30
ROYAL HAWAIIAN GIRLS' GLEE CLUB in Hulas and Songs 8:15 P. M.

On February 6, 1935, the Royal celebrated its eighth birthday with this large cake and some appropriately sized hula girls. HA

C. Stanford Cost, assistant manager of the Royal, was the first hotel manager in the United States to receive a hero's medal given by *Hotel Management Magazine*. He had rescued Dr. Pratt, a U.S. health officer in Honolulu, from the sea. Arthur G. Benaglia (right), manager of the Royal, presents Cost a trophy for his effort. HA

Christmas Dinner

Lichee Nut & Tangerine in Papaia

Consomme Royal   Queen & Jumbo Olives

Filet of Opakapaka Saute, Doria

Roast Stuffed Young Tom Turkey, Cranberry Sauce

Baked Virginia Ham, Champagne Sauce

Larded Filet of Beef

New Green Peas in Mint

Candied Yams   Mousseline Potatoes

Hearts of Lettuce, Roqueforte Dressing

Creme de Menthe Sherbet with Fruit Cake

Plum Pudding, Hard & Brandy Sauce

Hot Mince Pie

Pumpkin Pie

Cafe Noir

Assorted Nuts & Clustered Raisins

After Dinner Mints

Waialae Golf Club   *December 25, 1940*

Schedule of Holiday Events, 1940 - 41

AT THE ROYAL HAWAIIAN HOTEL

TUESDAY December 24th — Christmas Eve Dinner-Dance and Nite Club entertainment.   Lila Guerrero and the Hula Maid.

WEDNESDAY December 25th — Christmas Dinner and Classical Concert by Robin McQuesten's String Ensemble.

THURSDAY December 26th — Regular Dinner-Dance with Nite Club entertainment, on the Waikiki Terrace.

SATURDAY December 28th — Regular Dinner-Dance with Nite Club entertainment, on the Waikiki Terrace.

TUESDAY December 31st — Gala New Year's Eve Party. Kaaloa Notley, Royal Hawaiian Girls, The Islanders and others.

WEDNESDAY January 1st — New Year's Day Dinner and Classical Concert by Robin McQuesten's String Ensemble.

AT THE MOANA HOTEL

WEDNESDAY December 25th — Christmas Dinner and Hawaiian Concert by Royal Hawaiian Girls.

WEDNESDAY January 1st — New Year's Day Dinner and Hawaiian Concert by Royal Hawaiian Girls.

AT WAIALAE

WEDNESDAY December 25th — Christmas Dinner and Hawaiian entertainment, featuring Clara Inter and Joe Ikeole's Hawaiians. Dinner served 12:00 noon on. $2.00 per person.

FRIDAY December 27th — Regular Friday Dinner and Dance. Harry Owen's Orchestra featuring Clara Inter.

SUNDAY December 29th — Regular Sunday Dinner and Concert by Joe Ikeole's Hawaiians. Comic Hulas by Clara Inter.

TUESDAY December 31st — New Year's Eve Dinner and Dance. Entertainment by Joe Ikeole's Hawaiians 8 to 9 p. m. Dancing from 9 p.m. Ray Haley's Orchestra featuring Clara Inter.

To Our Patrons

Our kitchen is equipped to prepare any special dishes you may desire at moderate prices.

Parties & dinners with specially prepared menus can be arranged. Please leave your orders with our Maitre d'Hotel.

Kindly ask head waiter for souvenir menu ready for mailing.

The Waialae golf course at Waialae Beach offers you the finest 18 hole golf links in the Island. Green fee $2.00 on week days, $2.50 on Saturdays, Sundays & holidays. A completely equipped clubhouse. Weekly Dinner-dance every Friday. Special parties arranged.

A visit to the Pineapple cannery is interesting. Please see the Clerk at front office for details.

There are a number of beautiful & interesting automobile trips including a trip around the Island of Oahu. The Transportation Agent in the lobby will gladly furnish all information and make arrangements.

EVENTS OF THE DAY

HAWAIIAN SERENADERS   in the Dining Room   12:00 Noon
JOE KAMAKAU'S HAWAIIANS
COCONUT TREE CLIMBING by Hawaiian Boys -   2:30 P. M.
ROYAL HAWAIIAN GIRLS' GLEE CLUB   2:45 P. M.
ROYAL HAWAIIAN BAND & GLEE CLUB IN CONCERT 8:00 P. M.
DANCE IN THE BALLROOM   9:15 P. M.
The Brooks-McQuesten Orchestra

TEMPERATURES TODAY AIR 74 WATER 76

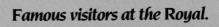

Gilbert Roland and Norma Talmadge, leading movie stars of the 1930s, were two of the countless stars who visited the Islands and stayed at the Royal. HA

Henry Ford and his first wife, Anne, spent part of their honeymoon at the Royal before flying to Hilo on Inter-Island Airways. HA

Sugar heiress, Geraldine Speckles, center, and her cousin, Lydin Griggs, enjoy a conversation with John Makua, head of the Royal Hawaiian Hotel beach patrol. HA

Peter Lawford, later to become a widely known actor, sits on the oceanside terrace with his parents, Gen. and Mrs. Sydney Lawford, in November 1934. Lawford would go on to a long acting career and a marriage into the Kennedy clan. HA

The famous comedy couple, George Burns and Gracie Allen, on the beach. HA

Australian pilot Charles Kingsford-Smith and his crew were greeted at the hotel on May 31, 1928. They made the first successful trans-Pacific flight from the mainland to Australia. RH

She was the most popular movie star of her day and all this before she was 10 years old. Shirley Temple made headlines when she visited Hawaii and the Royal in the mid-1930s. HA

Vice President Spiro Agnew and his entourage stayed at the hotel in the 1960s. RH

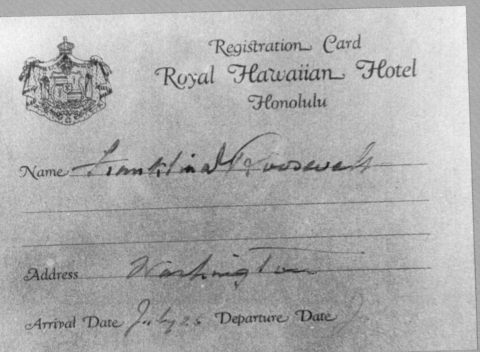

Registration Card
Royal Hawaiian Hotel
Honolulu

Name *Franklin D. Roosevelt*

Address *Washington*

Arrival Date *July 26* Departure Date

President Roosevelt visited Hawaii in July 1934, mainly for recreational purposes, and stayed at least one night at the Royal. U.S. Army Museum

CHAPTER SIX

Post-War to Modern

The Royal Hawaiian still was the dominant structure on this end of Waikiki Beach in 1968. Since then, a $50 million project resulted in construction of the 1,200-room Sheraton Waikiki Hotel, a 650-car parking garage and the 120-room Royal Hawaiian Tower. The Royal Hawaiian Shopping Center, built in the late 1970s, completed the encirclement of the old hotel. *Honolulu Star-Bulletin*

Post-War to Modern

"The elegant Royal Hawaiian Hotel has 555 air-conditioned rooms and suites. With its magnificent gardens, beach-front location, and superb dining, Hawaii's world-famous "Pink Palace" on Waikiki Beach offers the elegant and easygoing atmosphere of old Hawaii."

Royal Hawaiian Hotel Brochure

WHEN IT REOPENED IN 1947, The Royal Hawaiian again became the dominant luxury resort on Oahu. But the war had resulted in many changes in Hawaii's life and economy. Tourists again started coming to the Islands, this time on new, faster airplanes that cut flying time by many hours from the West Coast to Honolulu and that could carry many more passengers.

Now the tourists were different. With lower air fares and speedy travel, people of more modest means could enjoy the pleasures of the Islands during shorter stays. Smaller, less expensive hotels were starting to appear on or near Waikiki Beach. The Hawaii Visitors Bureau was becoming active in promoting Hawaii for both pleasure and conventions. It resumed production of the widely known radio program "Hawaii Calls" and advertised the Islands in mainland magazines. It sought to entice travelers to escape to "Paradise" and enjoy Hawaii's sun, sea and sand. The Royal would benefit from this intensive promotion in the next few decades.

In the 1950s, many new moderately priced hotels were built in the Waikiki area. Included were the SurfRider and the Princess Kaiulani, built by the Matson Company. As larger and faster planes reduced the flying time from the mainland to Hawaii, fewer and fewer vacationers wanted to spend 4½ days aboard a Matson ship each way. Although more than half of all the tourists who came to Hawaii in 1955 stayed in one of Matson's four hotels, only a fifth came by ship.

By 1959, jet service had reduced the flying time even more, which further eroded the steamers' business. It was a time of change for the old steamship company and it decided to divest itself of all non-shipping interests in the Islands and concentrate on the hauling of freight to and from the mainland and Hawaii.

After 32 years in the hotel business, the company in June 1959 sold its four hotels (Moana, Royal, SurfRider and Princess Kaiulani) to the Sheraton hotel chain for $17.6 million. At the time there was disagreement within Matson management over the sale. However, as Alexander Budge stated, "The hotels didn't make any money and were difficult for Matson to operate. There were constant problems in management and operations, and it was hard to keep on top of it."

Sheraton added the present 16-story Royal Tower Wing in 1969, bringing the combined room total to 526 (Royal Hawaiian and Royal Tower).

Sheraton in turn sold the Moana, SurfRider and Princess Kaiulani in 1963 to Kokusai Kogyo Co. Ltd., a Japanese company, for $30 million. In 1974, the Royal Hawaiian, Sheraton Maui and the Royal's next door neighbor, the newly built, 1,900-room Sheraton Waikiki Hotel, were sold for $105 million to Kyo-ya Co., Ltd., who has reinvested more than $35 million into the Royal since it was purchased. Sheraton continues to manage all the former Matson hotels under a contract with the owner, Kyo-ya Co., Ltd.

Today, the Royal still maintains its reputation for elegance, although the building itself has been overshadowed by the abundance of high-rises along the beach area. The Royal Hawaiian Shopping Center, built along Kalakaua Avenue in the late 1970s, finally closed off the original entrance to the Pink Palace. The hotel celebrated its 70th birthday and the 50th anniversary of its reopening in 1997.

Some of the original dishes and silver service from the Royal's opening night in 1927 are on display in the lower lobby. Island Camera

The Royal Hawaiian
day and night

The Royal Hawaiian
from oceanside

Coconut Grove Lanai

The Surf Room

Lobby

Garden and Porte Cochere

Hotel Staff

The Royal Hawaiian pool

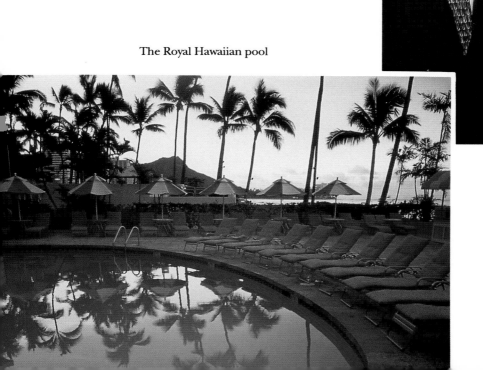

The Mai Tai Bar

Historic Ocean Room

Large Luxury Room

The Coconut Grove

A Historic Garden Room

In-Room Dining in a Garden Suite